"Our deepest fear is not that we are inadequate. Our deepest fear is that we are powerful beyond measure. It is our Light, not our darkness, that most frightens us....We are born to make manifest the Glory of God that is within us. It is not just some of us; it is everyone. And as we let our Light shine, we unconsciously give other people permission to do the same."

PRESIDENTIAL INAUGURATION
SPEECH OF NOBEL LAUREATE
NELSON MANDELA

With heartfelt gratitude to Bill Estell, Jacquie Kennedy, Karen Perkins, and Richard Carlston for their support and encouragement; to the talented artists whose creativity greatly enhanced this book; and to All.

158.1 FIN
Finney, Lynne D., 1941-
Windows to the light

Windows to the Light

Enriching Your Spirit with Haiku Meditations

Lynne D. Finney

with art by
Felix Saez
Norm Baker
Brady Donley
James Schnirel
G. Vernon Sears
Ben Schnirel
David C. Schultz
Jeanne S. Lindorff
Rafael Reynal
Skip Huntress
Paul Thiessen
Mark Lukes

PARK CITY LIBRARY
1255 Park Avenue
P.O. Box 668
Park City, Utah 84060
Phone: (435) 615-5600

Changes Publishing

C. 1
16.00
12/02

Windows to the Light:
Enriching Your Spirit with Haiku Meditations.

Copyright © 2001 by Lynne D. Finney with art by Felix Saez, Brady Donley, James Schnirel, G. Vernon Sears, Ben Schnirel, Norm Baker, David C. Schultz, Jeanne S. Lindorff, Rafael Reynal, Skip Huntress, Paul Thiessen, and Mark Lukes. Printed in the United States of America.

All rights reserved. This book may not be reproduced in whole or in part without written permission from the publisher, except by a reviewer who may quote brief passages in a review; nor many any part of this book be reproduced, stored in a retrieval system, or transmitted in any form or by any means, electronic, mechanical, photo-copying, recording, or other, without written permission from the publisher. For information contact Changes Publishing, P.O. Box 681539, Park City, UT 84068-1539.

Cover art: Norm Baker, Riverdale, Utah
Cover design and interior layout: Sunset Graphics, Roy, Utah
Printing: Profile Media, Provo, Utah

FIRST EDITION

ISBN 0-9625883-1-8

22 21 20 19 18 17 16 15 14 13 12 11 10 9 8 7 6 5 4 3 2 1

Body or spirit?
Are we separate or One?
Particles or waves?

INTRODUCTION

The earliest poems were songs, prayers, and incantations to the gods. Poetry is inherently spiritual, pulling us into a greater awareness of beauty and truth.

"Haiku" is a Japanese word for a type of contemplative poetry, the medium of oriental mystics. For centuries, the Japanese have used haiku for meditation, as part of their spiritual practice.

Many of these haiku came to me in a mystical way. About five years ago, I woke up at 5 a.m. and was propelled downstairs to my computer. I had never written a haiku, or any poetry other than childish rhymes in elementary school. For three days, haiku poured out of me.

Without knowing why, I spontaneously used three lines with 5, 7, and 5 syllables. Writing haiku was fun, totally different from the self-help books I'd been writing, and I found myself chuckling as I typed. It was a diverting challenge, like fitting together pieces of a puzzle.

Later I discovered that the three-line stanza I'd used is the traditional haiku form. I joked with friends that I must have channeled a samurai warrior.

Years after writing many of these haiku, I learned that Basho, recognized as the greatest of haiku poets, had been a samurai warrior. During the seventeenth century, Basho imbued the form with the spirit of Zen Buddhism, attempting to compress the meaning of the world into the simple pattern of his poetry - a goal I too had unconsciously pursued. These haiku are the result of decades of studying various religions, scriptures and spiritual teachings, as well as psychology and healing techniques, and of profound spiritual experiences.

Haiku continue to pop into my head, seeming to arise from something larger than myself. This phenomenon no longer seems strange because I've come to see that we have an unlimited ability to tap into all the knowledge of the universe, the collective consciousness described by psychiatrist Carl Jung.

Ancient Japanese haiku focused on nature and images of the four seasons, but today haiku are written in many languages and cover a broad range of subjects. Although many of my haiku are nontraditional with images from the modern world, such as computers and quantum physics, I like to think that Basho is my muse. The idea that a samurai warrior would choose as his channel a liberated woman in sweats typing at a computer - a far cry from a geisha - gives me a good laugh.

My wish is that these haiku help you, as they helped me, to plumb the depths of your mind and awaken to your true self and the miracles around you. You don't have to know anything about haiku. There is no right or wrong way to read or interpret them. Just play.

There are many ways of using haiku for meditation. One way is to read each haiku slowly by itself. Enjoy the art and ask yourself how it adds to your insights. Avoid rushing through the pages; read one haiku and think about it during the day. These haiku and the artwork are designed to surprise, startle, and even shock you into new perceptions.

If you have a few minutes to practice more formal meditation, sit comfortably and take some deep, gentle breaths before reading a haiku. You can close your eyes or focus on the words or art. Then allow your mind to wonder and wander freely. This is a time for what ifs, for escaping limitations, for impossible imaginings - recognizing that nothing you can imagine is impossible. Simply allow thoughts, images, or insights to float into your mind. Whatever happens is right for you.

Keeping a journal of your thoughts may also be helpful. It can inspire you to write your own haiku and to see life through new eyes.

The insights and answers you need come from your own mind. You are designed to awaken; that's your purpose. Whatever path you are on is exactly where you are supposed to be at this moment. There are no mistakes, only lessons to help you grow. You can't fail spirituality because you are spirit. You are a precious part of a perfect plan.

As a follower of Zen Buddhism, Basho might have been familiar with my favorite quote, attributed to the Buddha: "If you search the wide world over, you will never find anyone more deserving of love than yourself."

My prayer is that you find love, peace, and your true self - and experience the Radiance surrounding you and in you.

Love and blessings,

Lynne

On a vision quest,
we're trying to get back Home.
But we never left.

Yesterday has died.
Tomorrow is a mirage.
Why do I worry?

The world is its own
magic, and each of us a
unique Houdini.

Clown-faced puffins strut
proudly, comic creations
of a playful god.

The fish is thirsty
and we are searching for God.
Cosmic comedy!

Some days I can't see
the love, help, and miracles
that are always here.

The universe is
perfectly orchestrated;
there are no mistakes.

Hidden within us
is a bud of light we are
here to make blossom.

A thousand stained glass
windows spiral to the sun -
butterflies swarming.

We are blind and deaf,
but when we become aware,
miracles appear.

Dancing through darkness,
I trust there are infinite
windows to the light.

Snowflakes swirl around
my body, filling the globe
of my perception.

Astronauts gaze at
the blue marble of our world
and become mystics.

Inside us is a small
still voice, soft as the whisper
of a willow tree.

Wart hogs wallowing
in slime are as loved by God
as are hummingbirds.

The scent of blossoms
encircles my soul forming
a lei of welcome.

To live is holy,
just to be is a blessing,
to be is enough.

A marmot basking,
copper fur on copper rocks,
has no fears or wants.

Unconditional
love also includes yourself.
Fill your own cup first.

You are the only
problem you will ever have --
and the solution!

Look back at your life.
Can you see disasters that
grew into blessings?

The Universe wants
to give us everything good.
We push it away.

This is a drama
that seems real; pause and observe
what is in your mind.

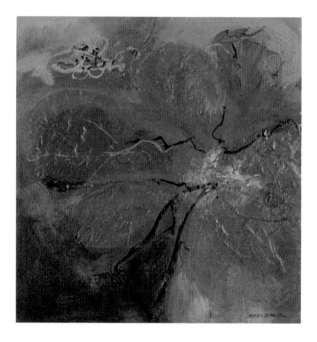

Child, God is in you
just as fragrance and color
are in a flower.

Be still and listen
to the restless wind, a stone,
the small voice within.

You are the only
person in your lifetime who
will never leave you.

Renouncing my search
for a partner to be whole,
I find that I am.

Love is the lotus
unfolding its pink softness
to reveal the source.

Coincidence is
simply God's way of showing
us S/He is around.

No matter what you've
done or what was done to you,
you are always pure.

No matter what you've
done or what was done to you,
you can always heal.

No matter what you've
done or what was done to you,
you are loved by God.

You are forgiven
no matter what you have done.
Now pardon yourself.

Cold snowy blanket,
whiteness of a slate wiped clean.
All is forgiven.

Tiny particles
create us every moment,
endlessly changing.

We are all equal,
just in different stages
of our shared journey.

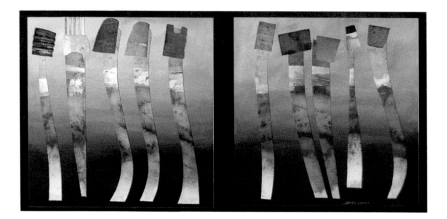

Since I am spirit,
how can I be sick, tired,
or apart from Love?

Worms have a purpose.
They don't see what it is but
do it by being.

Bright parkas swirling,
parallel tracks in soft snow
carving paths of joy.

Minds and stars are born,
planets whirl, porpoises play;
the universe breathes.

A bird, AIDS baby,
terrorist, and Buddha all
show us the way Home.

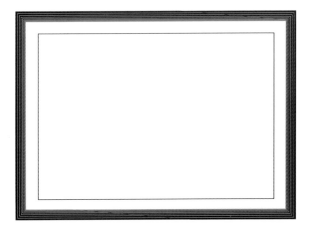

We're one with spirit,
all dancing in the circle
that has no ending.

We sit at keyboards
clicking mice, blind to souls caught
in the world wide web.

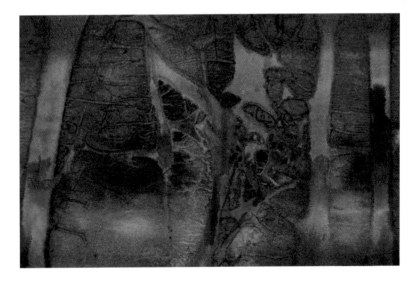

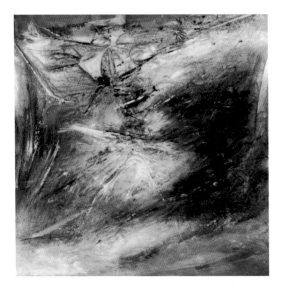

How can we share more
beauty as we dance our lives
on this spinning star?

The prickly thistle
becomes a purple flower,
then soars as soft down.

Filled with ancient fears,
my heart is walled within me.
Will Love pierce my shell?

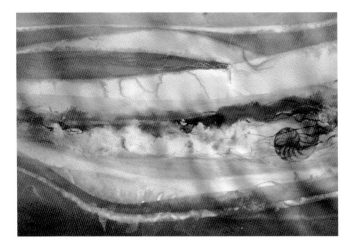

You are divinely
guided; the path you take is
always the right path

A butterfly and
a hippopotamus play
in such different ways.

When I face my fears,
the past dissolves like cobwebs,
spiders brought to light.

I cherish my pain
as a fire that burns away
what keeps me from Love.

A red drop of blood
on the green leaf flies away -
ladybug goes home.

Some people march to
a different drummer, and
some people polka.

Rowdy crows gorge on
Kansas corn, blind to famine
in the Sahara.

Gold eyes in white fur
gaze at me with total trust;
I can do no wrong.

Living stars of gold,
scarlet and orange swirl in
kaleidoscope shapes.

Eagles soar above
the illusion, observing
the shadows below.

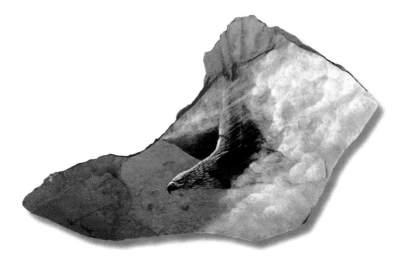

You were created
by the same Divine Love that
created Buddha.

You were created
by the same Divine Love that
created Jesus.

You were created
by the same Divine Love that
created Krishna.

You were created
by the same Divine Love that
created Hitler.

Genes, stars and rainbows
are cosmic variations
of a loving Mind.

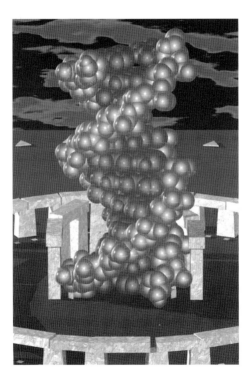

Tulips, sage, and pines
sprout through fertile loam as I
stroll on holy ground.

A golden eagle
flies free above the rainbow,
cradled in Love's light.

Flocks of chickadees
on snow drifts peck red berries,
chirping Love's carols.

All sea life depends
on plankton too small to see;
all life is sacred.

A golden jonquil bows
then lifts her chin, savoring
her precious moments.

When the sun rises,
a child is born, a rose blooms,
we feel reverence.

Snow falls as silent
forests sleep. Is that the sound
of one hand clapping?

All beings we meet
are guardian angels with
messages of grace.

Ghostly petroglyphs,
dancing dreams on sunny cliffs,
defy extinction.

Shimmering aspens,
golden streaks across the hills,
painting summer's death.

Dandelion wisps
sail gently upwards to the sun
like departing souls.

All rivers flow to
the same ocean; why not go
directly to God?

Larks sing, eagles soar,
trout leap. The universe is
a celebration!

A symphony of
rustling leaves lulls me into
harmony with All.

We're like porcupines
trying to be close and warm
without being hurt.

When I surrender,
the universe guides my path.
My life is perfect.

You can't see plankton
with your eye; without them you'll
have no fish to fry.

If you were not here,
a color would be missing
in the Tapestry.

Be sure your ladder
of success is not leaning
against the wrong wall.

Since intention molds
our reality, why not
intend happiness?

Creatures of the sea
swim in an endless cycle -
predator and prey.

We walk through forests
of physical things, missing
the spirit within.

Following our bliss,
we flow with the endless source
of abundant love.

A harvest moon shines
gold on wings of snowy owls
swooping toward their prey.

Bluebird, were you formed
to show me happiness is
in my own backyard?

If the only prayer
you ever say is "thank you,"
that one will suffice.

Your thumb is unique.
No one has ever had or
will have your thumb print.

In crystal dewdrops,
clear reflections of tide pools
and oceans beyond.

A thousand times a
thousand paths to nirvana -
all roads take us home.

Humans are crazy;
we can't make a worm but make
gods by the dozens.

We are more space than
matter, believing we are
solid. Illusion.

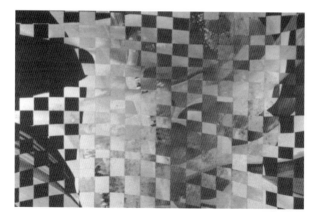

Shadowy branches
shimmer through dancing snowflakes:
gossamer mirage.

I'm stroking tan skin,
spice scented, glad that Love made
our love tangible.

A flower and its
fertilizer are all part
of the Radiance.

God is not found by
adding something to a soul,
but by subtracting.

We see things as two:
man-woman, substance-shadow,
body-spirit. ONE.

Duality is
illusion; no bad, no good,
there is only Love.

We co-create with
God; risk and make your life a
work of living art.

Peel away layers
of an onion and you'll find
nothing....Everything.

Peel off your beliefs
like layers of an onion,
and find your true Self.

Not flesh, fears, or thoughts,
My true Self never changes.
Who asks "Who am I?"

You will never find
anyone more deserving
of love than yourself.

I AM only Love.
I AM the whole universe.
I AM THAT I AM.

ABOUT THE AUTHOR

Lynne D. Finney, J.D., M.S.W. – author and photographer

Haiku and photographs on pages 8, 12, 16, 18, 29, 35, 42, 60, 66, 69, 85, 93, and 94.

Lynne is an award-winning author, educator, lawyer, and retired psychotherapist who presents transformation, creativity, empowerment and writers classes and workshops across the country. A former radio talk show host, Lynne has appeared as a guest on over 100 radio and television shows throughout the United States and Canada, including three times on Larry King's shows.

As a child, Lynne had three near-death experiences during abuse. Low self-esteem drove her to overachieve and become a corporate attorney, law professor, counsel to a U.S. Senator, diplomat, and U.S. delegate. President Carter appointed Lynne as the first woman director of a federal banking agency and to White House Task Forces.

Lynne spent decades studying the most effective psychological and spiritual techniques for healing and transformation and became a psychotherapist to pass on what she learned. She began to have spiritual experiences that opened her to new perceptions of reality and emerged from a world she perceived as hell into a world of miracles.

Lynne's first book, *Reach for the Rainbow; Advanced Healing for Survivors of Sexual Abuse*, became a classic in the field, followed by *Reach for Joy; How to Find the Right Therapist and Therapy for You*. *Clear Your Past, Change Your Future* reveals the techniques Lynne used in her own healing and foreign editions have been published in India, Spain, and Russia, and soon in Chinese. *Clearing Your Past* is a recent audio package of Lynne's workshops and contains a unique guided meditation for connecting with the Universe.

As a photographer, Lynne is an amateur. It took four rolls of film to get acceptable photographs of dandelions, onions, and thistle, but she loves to capture nature's miracles and play in Utah's mountains. c/o Changes Publishing, P.O. Box 681539, Park City, UT 84068 email lynne@lynnefinney.com, www.lynnefinney.com.

ABOUT THE ARTISTS

Felix Saez – sculptor and painter

Pages 7, 17, 23, 48, 51, 53, 57, 63, 64, 68, 72, 75, and 79.

Born in Bingham Canyon, Utah, Felix became aware of artistic ability at an early age. While raising his family of two children in Arizona and later Utah, he was encouraged to pursue his art career full time. Felix has experience in many media, inducing graphic and silk screen design, murals, and carving. Now he focuses on acrylic painting and relief carvings of Native Americans and wildlife. His unique art is created using the natural contours, fractures, and colors in the stones he carefully selects – sandstone and quartzite from Utah, Idaho, and Arizona, and slate from as far away as India. He sees his images in the stone before beginning to paint or sculpt.

Felix's work has been exhibited extensively throughout the United States and is now in the Stone Art Gallery in Park City, Utah; The Gallery at Park City; Paseo Gallery, Park City; Wyland Galleries, Las Vegas, Nevada and South Lake Tahoe, California; Quest Gallery, Banff, Canada; Northwoods Gallery, Land-O-Lakes, Wisconsin; and Canvas Cowboys Gallery, Riverside, Washington. His work has been commissioned by galleries, non-profit organizations, and individuals such as actor Chuck Norris and Roy of Siegfried & Roy. He even did a portrait of the MGM Lion "Metro" and a sandstone sculpture of the famous actor bear "Bart".

4915 West Ponderosa Drive, Park City, UT 84098, (801) 856-7538, email felix@fineartonstone.com, www.fineartonstone.com

Brady Donley – photographer

Pages 2, 4, 5, 14, 15, 32, 34, 37, 45, 59, 61, 76, 78, 80, 88, and 92.

Brady is an internationally recognized commercial photographer, whose passion for photographing wildlife has taken him around the world in search of the perfect picture. He has traveled to all seven continents, photographing penguins in Antarctica, whale sharks off the coast of Australia, and lions on the Serengeti plains in East Africa. Brady graduated from the University of Utah with a B.F. A. in photography and has owned a custom photo lab for more than a dozen years.

Brady's photographs have been exhibited in galleries in

San Francisco and Park City, Utah and published in magazines such as *Architectural Digest* and *Great Lakes Golf Magazine*. His work is in collections in the United States, Germany, Tanzania, and England. His photographs for Microsoft appear in the Links computer games.
(801) 466-8625, Fax (801) 484-2924, email Bdonley@inconnect.com.

James Schnirel – watercolorist

Pages 20, 24, 33, 36, 40, 41, 43, 44, 62, 77, 83, 84, and 86.

Jim's work is infinitely creative and varied, ranging from abstracts and murals to landscapes, flowers, and mystical. Born in the lake country of Geneva, New York, his early years were spent drawing, painting, and woodworking. After graduating from the School of Architecture at the University of Oklahoma in 1959, he earned a Master of Science degree at Utah State University, and became a college teacher, administrator, and finally vice president for administration. Retired in 1987 to pursue painting full time, Jim now also teaches watercolor painting and conducts workshops to keeps his spontaneity flowing.

Jim's paintings have been exhibited in Utah, Arizona, New Mexico, Colorado, and Taipei, China. He has won cash awards and honors and has had several one-man shows, including a show at the nationally-acclaimed Kimball Art Center in Park City, Utah. His work has been acquired by private collectors, corporations, schools and colleges in the United States, Germany, Switzerland, Sweden and Denmark.
P.O. Box 311, Moab, UT 84532.

G. Vernon Sears - photographer

Pages 10, 19, 22, 26, 27, 47, 50, 70, 74, 82, 90, and 91.

G. Vernon had a fascination for photography since he was a boy. In his early thirties, he was inspired by an exhibit of Edward Weston's photographs to work with large format cameras and black and white photography. Working with natural light and shadow to transform ordinary scenes into works of art, G. Vernon spends months in the Great Salt Lake Desert, the Black Rock Desert in Nevada, and the Sonora Desert.

His photographs have been exhibited in juried shows and two were purchased by the University of Utah Museum of Fine Arts for its permanent collection.
2225 Fardown Avenue, Holladay, Utah 84121, (801) 272-2225, e-mail gvernonsears@webtv.net

Ben Schnirel – painter

Pages 1, 21, 25, 39, 56, and 73.

A professional artist for more than 15 years, Ben works with oils, acrylic, and gouache. He captures the magnificent scenery of the desert Southwest in vibrant colors. His work is exhibited in galleries and art museums.

Ben's paintings hang in public buildings and have been commissioned by collectors and colleges. He was a winner in the U.S. Department of the Interior's "Art for the Parks" competition.

P.O. Box 311, Moab, UT 84532, (435) 259-2386

Norm Baker – photographer

Cover and pages 3, 6, 46, 67, 71, 81, 87, and 95.

Norm Baker is a native of Utah with a great love for both the State and photographing it. He won top ribbons at the Weber County Fair and received awards for his work at the Utah State Fair.

His photographs have been included in the Utah Arts Council State Wide Exhibition. He is a past president of the Ogden Camera Club.

4261 South 800 West, Riverdale, UT 84405, (801) 621-2509, email normbaker@qwest.com

David C. Schultz – photographer

Pages 31, 49, 65, and 89.

A native of Michigan, David first became interested in photography when he purchased a camera to record his travels after high school. Beginning as a commercial photographer, he later expanded to fashion photography for regional and national publications and clothing designers. While on assignment in Utah, David realized how much he missed the outdoors, closed his studio in Texas, and moved to the Wasatch mountains to pursue a rekindled love for landscape photography.

David's commercial work continues and his photographs are represented by several stock agencies around the world. His images have appeared internationally in such publications as *National Geographic Traveler* and *Travel and Leisure*. His work has been exhibited in numerous galleries, as well as his own gallery in Park City, Utah, and a book of his photographs has been published.

West Light Images, P.O. Box 680331, Park City, UT 84068-0331, (435) 645-8414, www.westlight.net

Jeanne S. Lindorff – watercolorist

Page 28.

Jeanne is a long-time commercial artist, a member of the Utah Watercolor Society, and her work has been exhibited in Utah. (801) 278-9662.

Rafael Reynal – photographer

Page 9.

A native of Argentina, Rafael has lived and studied in the United States. While in Santa Cruz, California, he photographed the monarch butterflies swarming on their migration south.
Cervino 3974 Piso 3 (C1425AGV), Buenos Aires, Argentina

Skip Huntress – photographer

Page 11.

Skip specializes in portraiture, advertising, and interiors and has a studio in Salt Lake City.
1223 E. Roosevelt Avenue, Salt Lake City, UT 84105,
(801) 487-8850, www.skiphuntress.com

Paul Thiessen – photographer and graphic artist.

Page 55.

Paul is freelance photographer who creates custom molecular and chemical graphics. He combines DNA graphics with creative themes such as the Stonehenge background used in this book.
www.chemicalgraphics.com

NASA – Page 13. http://visibleearth.nasa.gov/

Mark Lukes, Sunset Graphics – graphic artist and designer

Cover design, interior layout, and computer creations on pages 29, 38, 58, and 85.

Sunset Graphics is the creation of artist and computer wizard Mark Lukes and has quickly attracted major corporate clients and small businesses in Utah and nationally. Mark has experience in printing and advertising and Sunset Graphics is known for its high quality designs and layouts in publications from art books to brochures.
4802 South 4075 West, Roy, Utah 84067, (801) 725-4552
email snstgrfx@earthlink.net.